OXFORD
UNIVERSITY PRESS

Oxford International Primary History

Workbook

Helen Crawford

1

Oxford International Primary for enquiring minds

OXFORD

OXFORD
UNIVERSITY PRESS

Great Clarendon Street, Oxford, OX2 6DP, United Kingdom

Oxford University Press is a department of the University of Oxford.
It furthers the University's objective of excellence in research,
scholarship, and education by publishing worldwide. Oxford is a
registered trade mark of Oxford University Press in the UK and in
certain other countries.

British Library Cataloguing in Publication Data
Data available

ISBN: 978-0-19-841815-3

10 9 8 7 6

Paper used in the production of this book is a natural, recyclable
product made from wood grown in sustainable forests. The
manufacturing process conforms to the environmental regulations
of the country of origin.

Printed in India by Manipal Technologies Limited

Acknowledgements

Cover illustration: Carlo Molinari

Illustrations: Aptara

Although we have made every effort to trace and contact all
copyright holders before publication this has not been possible in all
cases. If notified, the publisher will rectify any errors or omissions at
the earliest opportunity.

Contents

What do I already know?

Read the questions in the speech bubbles. Tell a friend your ideas.

How are you similar to other people?

How are you different from other people?

How have you changed since you were a baby?

How have you stayed the same since you were a baby?

Who are all the different people in your family?

Look at the pictures of Ahmed on pages 4–5 of your Student Book.

1 Copy the picture that shows Ahmed when he is youngest.

How do you know Ahmed is youngest in this picture?

_____

2 Copy the picture that shows Ahmed when he is oldest.

How do you know Ahmed is oldest in this picture?

_____

All about me!

1 Draw a picture of yourself in the box.

2 Complete the speech bubbles.

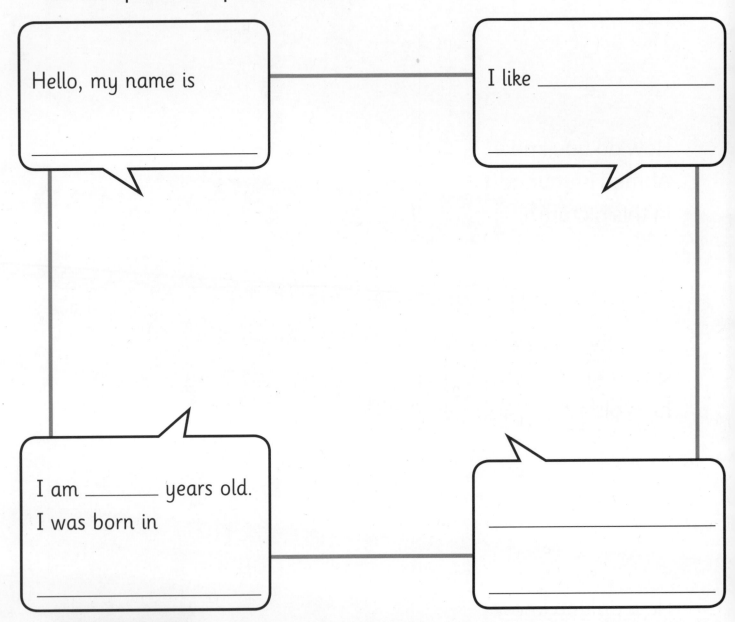

Hello, my name is _____

I like _____

I am _____ years old.
I was born in _____

Challenge

Write one more sentence all about you inside the empty speech bubble.

Similar or different?

1 Draw a picture of
   your friend.

2 Complete the
   sentences.

I am similar to my friend because _____

_____

We are different because _____

_____

Older or younger?

Three people who are **older** than me	Three people who are **younger** than me
My teacher	

When I was a baby

Put ✓ next to the things that are for a baby. Put ✗ next to the things that are not for a baby. The first one has been done for you.

How have I changed?

When I was a baby	Now I am _____ years old
I drank	I drink
I ate	I eat
I wore	I wear
I slept in a	I sleep in a

How have I stayed the same?

Talk to an adult at home. Find out all the ways you have stayed the same since you were a baby.

Mia's timeline

Draw a line to link each picture to the correct part of the timeline.

0 years

2 years

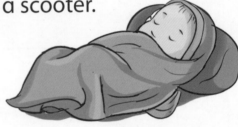

I rode a scooter.

I was born.

4 years

I went to school.

6 years

I drew a picture.

What is a timeline?

Choose words from the box to complete the sentences.

order	past
timeline	events

A _____ shows when something happened

in the _____ .

A timeline helps us to put _____ in the correct

_____ .

My timeline

1 Look at photos of yourself when you were different ages.

2 Draw yourself at different ages on the timeline below.

A family tree

Use the words in the box to complete Ahmed's family tree.

mother	father	grandfather
grandmother	grandmother	sister
grandfather		

Ahmed

Different generations

Three people who are in the **same** generation as me	Three people who are in an **older** generation than me
1 My friend	1
2	2
3	3

My family tree

1 Draw your family tree on a piece of paper. Ask an adult to help you.

Include: grandparents, parents, uncles, aunts, sisters, brothers and cousins.

2 Bring your family tree into school.

1.5 What can we learn from a photo?

What has changed?

Look at the pictures.

1 Draw pictures to show what these objects look like today.

2 Write a label for each picture.

In the past

Today

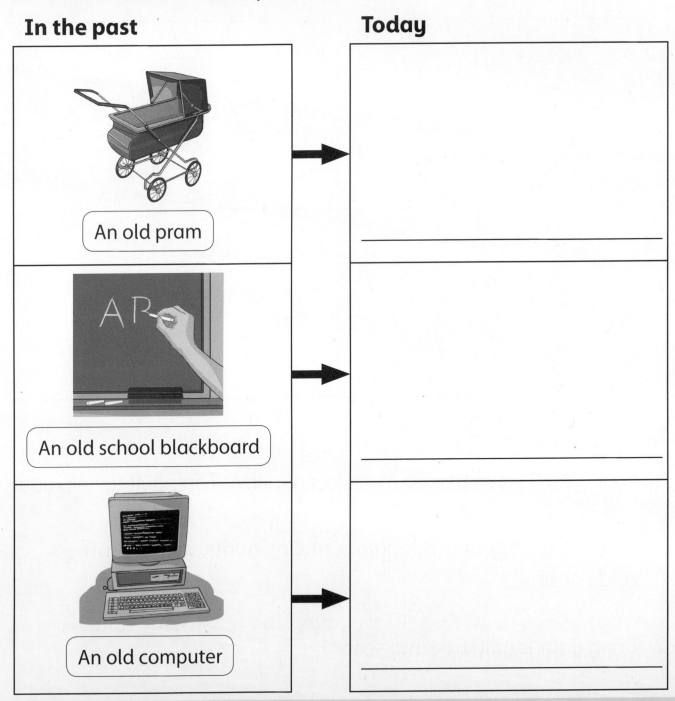

An old pram

An old school blackboard

An old computer

My family history

Look at a photo that was taken before you were born and shows someone in your family. Draw a picture of the photo or stick the photo in the box. Answer the questions about the photo.

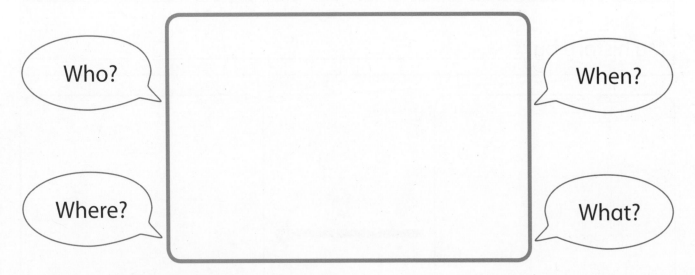

Who?

When?

Where?

What?

1 Who is in the photo?

_____

2 Where was the photo taken?

_____

3 When was the photo taken?

_____

4 What is happening in the photo?

_____

Challenge

What does this photo tell you about the past? Write your answer in your notebook.

1 Thinking about my learning

My history

Complete this page about your history.

My history by _____

This is me as a baby.

This is me today.

Write about your family.

This is my family.

Thinking about my learning

Learning outcome I can...	☺	😐	☹
talk about history as a study of the past.			
describe how I have changed over time.			
describe how I have stayed the same.			
talk about how I am similar to and different from other people.			

Three things I have learned...

1 _____

2 _____

3 _____

My favourite activity was...

_____

_____

My favourite fact was...

_____

_____

What do I already know?

Read the questions in the speech bubbles. Tell a friend your ideas.

What is a house?

What are the different rooms inside a house?

What does an old house look like?

What does a modern house look like?

What does your house look like?

Look at the pictures of different doors on page 19 of your Student Book.

1 Copy a picture of an old door.

How do you know this is an old door?

_____

_____

_____

_____

_____

_____

2 Copy a picture of a new door.

How do you know this is a new door?

_____

_____

_____

_____

_____

Let's look outside

Look at the houses. Label the different parts of each house.
Use the words in the box. One has been done for you.

| roof | door | window | wall | chimney |

A modern house

window

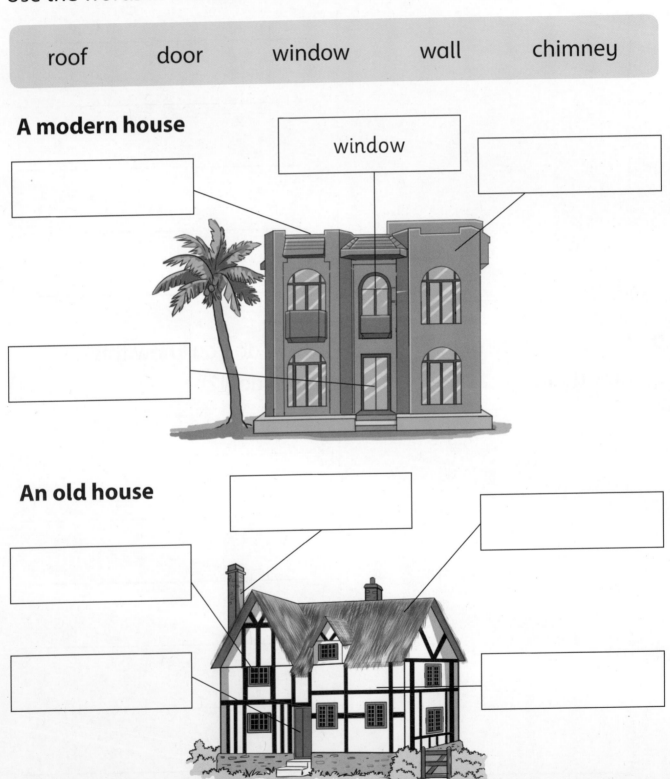

An old house

Houses in my local area

Go for a walk around your local area. Look at all the houses.

1 Draw a picture of one house.

2 Label the different parts of the house. Use the words in the box on page 20.

1 Is the house you have drawn modern or old?

_____

2 How is this house similar to the old house on page 20?

_____

3 How is this house different from the old house on page 20?

_____

Old or modern?

Look at the pictures.

Put ✓ if the object is from an old kitchen. Put ✗ if the object is from a modern kitchen. The first one has been done for you.

A microwave

This is from an old kitchen. ✓

A coal bucket

This is from an old kitchen. ☐

A stove

This is from an old kitchen. ☐

An electric kettle

This is from an old kitchen. ☐

A kettle

This is from an old kitchen. ☐

A food mixer

This is from an old kitchen. ☐

Heating the stove

1 Look at this picture of a stove. Draw someone using bellows to heat the stove.

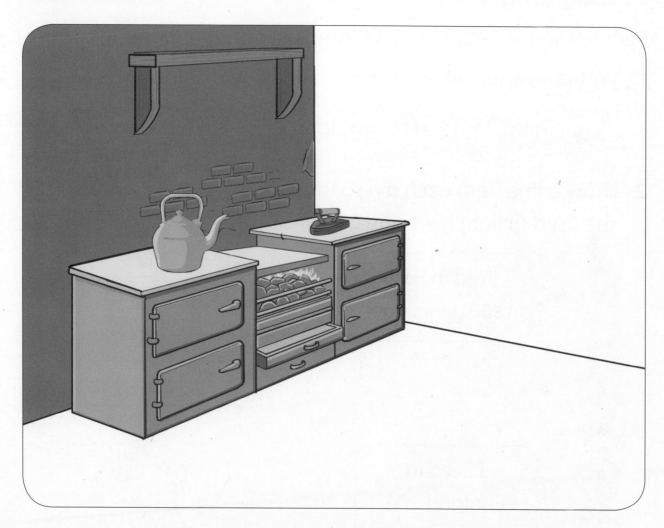

2 Choose words from the box to complete the sentences.

hotter	bellows	air	stove

The _____ blew _____ on to

the fire. The air made the fire _____.

The fire heated the _____.

Putting lamps in time order

People used different kinds of lamps at different times in the past.

1 Write the name of each lamp. Use the words in the box.

oil lamp	gas lamp	electric lamp

2 Draw a line from each girl to the lamp she used to light her house.

I lived in Rome 1800 years ago.

_____

I lived in England 200 years ago.

_____

I live now.

_____

Electric lights

Modern houses have electric lights. Put ✓ next to the lights that use electricity. Put ✗ next to the lights that do not use electricity. The first one has been done for you.

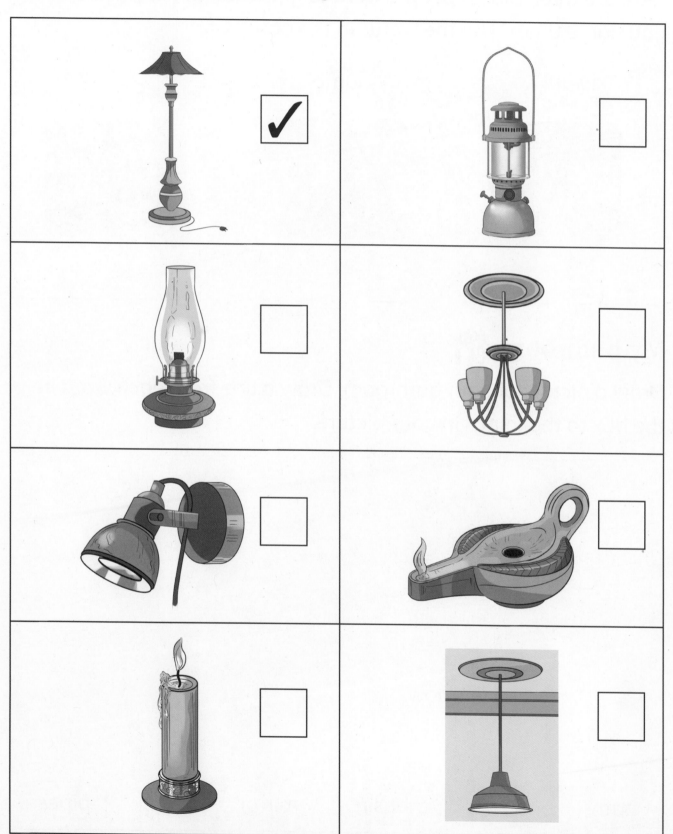

Finding water

Here are three places people went to get water in the past. Can you name them? Use the words in the box.

| well | pump | river |

My bathroom

Draw a picture of your bathroom. Draw a line from each word in the box to the things in your picture.

bath   shower   basin   mirror   tap   pipes

Looking at adverts

This toothpaste advert is 100 years old.

1 Design a modern advert for toothpaste.
   You could include pictures of:

   • a modern bathroom

   • someone brushing their teeth.

Name of your toothpaste:

Draw your advert here.

2 Complete the sentences.

   My advert is similar to the old advert because...

   _____

   My advert is different from the old advert because...

   _____

Washing day objects

These objects were used on washing day in the past. Match the pictures with the words. The first one has been done for you.

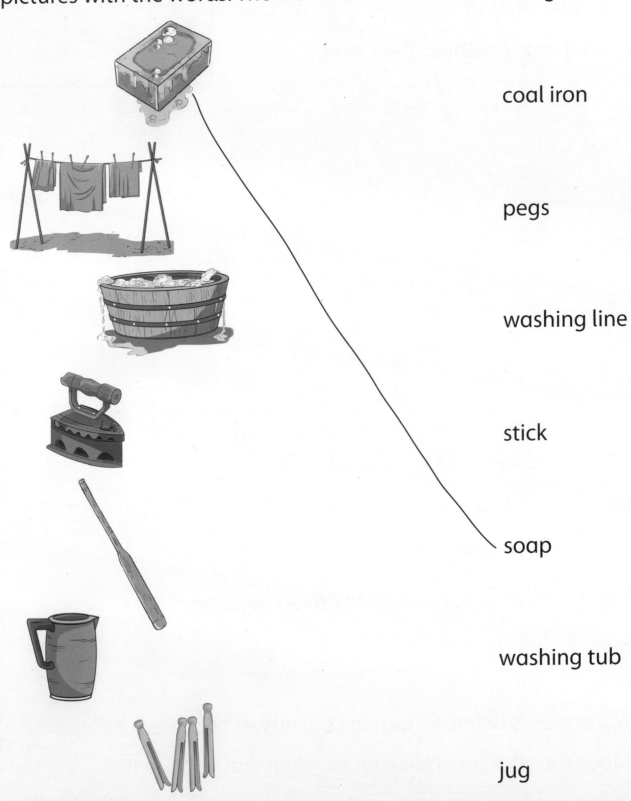

coal iron

pegs

washing line

stick

soap

washing tub

jug

Washing clothes in the past

Write the numbers from 1–6 to order how clothes were washed, dried and ironed in the past. Number 1 has been done for you.

Peg the clothes on the washing line.

Put the clothes in the tub.

Rub the clothes with soap.

Iron the clothes.

Move the stick up and down.

1 Put water in the tub.

What were houses like long ago?

What were houses like long ago? Write your ideas inside the house shape.

What were
houses like long ago?

Challenge

Why have houses changed over time? Write your ideas in your notebook.

Thinking about my learning

Learning outcome I can... ·	☺	😐	☹
compare old and modern houses.			
order household objects on a timeline.			
describe how houses have changed over time.			

Three things I have learned...

1 _____

2 _____

3 _____

My favourite activity was...

_____

_____

My favourite fact was...

_____

_____

What do I already know?

Look at the pictures of the three explorers on pages 32–33 of your Student Book.

Read the questions in the speech bubbles here.

Tell a friend your ideas.

What is an explorer?

Can you name any famous explorers?

How do people travel around the world today?

How did people travel around the world in the past?

Would you like to be an explorer?

Look at these pictures of the three explorers. Answer the questions.

Ibn Battuta

Christopher Columbus

Edmund Hillary

1 What animal is Ibn Battuta riding?

_____

What does this tell you about the places he explored?

_____

2 What is Christopher Columbus holding in his hand?

_____

What does this tell you about the places he explored?

_____

3 What is Edmund Hillary holding in his hand?

_____

What does this tell you about the places he explored?

_____

Ibn Battuta

This is a map of Ibn Battuta's journeys.

1 Colour the land brown. Colour the oceans and seas blue.

2 Draw a line from each label to the correct object on the map. The first one has been done for you.

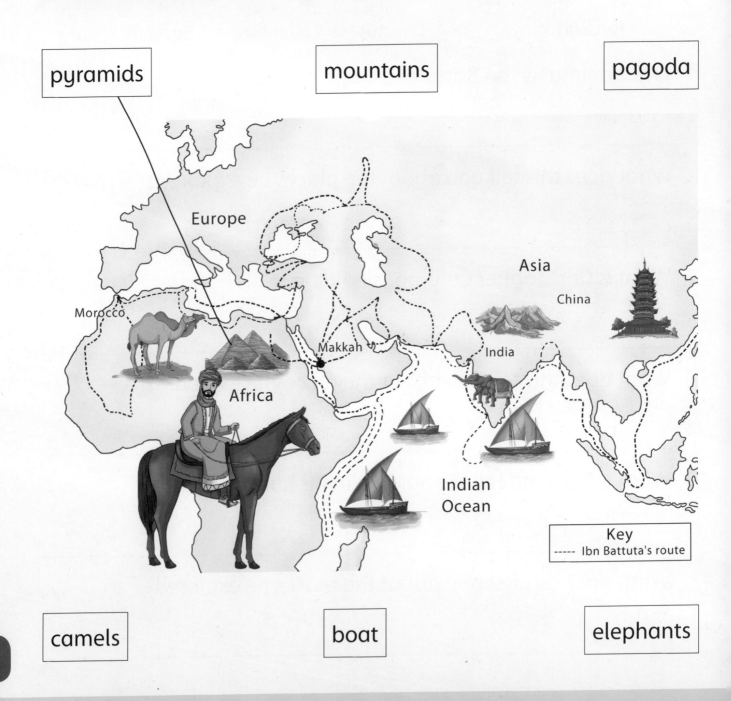

pyramids

mountains

pagoda

camels

boat

elephants

Key
----- Ibn Battuta's route

Going on a journey

Think about a journey you have made.

1 Write answers to these questions about your journey.

Where did you go? _____

Who did you go with? _____

How did you travel? _____

What did you see?

_____

_____

2 Draw a picture of something you saw on your journey.

A voyage

Christopher Columbus sailed for 70 days. The voyage across the Atlantic Ocean was dangerous. Write a sentence in each sailor's speech bubble. Use the words in the box to help you.

| scared | hungry | water |
| tired | food | voyage |

A new land

Sailors use a log book to write about their voyages. You are Christopher Columbus. You are in a new land. What can you see? How do you feel? Complete your log book.

A new land   1492

I can see _____

_____

_____

I feel _____

_____

_____

Special clothes

It is very cold on Mount Everest. There is snow and ice.

1 Colour the clothes Edmund Hillary wore to climb Mount Everest.

2 There is some space in the suitcase. Draw one more item of clothing Edmund Hillary wore to climb Mount Everest.

3 Write a label for the item you have drawn.

Snow boots

Sun hat

Snow goggles

Mittens

Shorts

Flipflops

Famous!

1 Read this newspaper story. Fill in the missing words. Use the words in the box.

2 Write a headline for the story and draw a picture.

Norgay	Everest	famous	1953
snow	Nepal	dangerous	Zealand

The Nepal News   Saturday 30th May 1953

Write your headline here.

On 29th May _____ Edmund

Hillary climbed to the top of

Mount _____. He

climbed with Tenzing _____.

Draw a picture here.

Edmund Hillary is from New _____. Tenzing

Norgay is from _____. The journey was very

_____. The two men climbed in

_____ and ice. Now they are

_____ across the world.

3.4 Who was the bravest explorer?

Brave explorers

Read the speech bubbles. Draw a line to match each speech bubble to the correct explorer. The first one has been done for you.

I went to the South Pole.

I rode on an elephant.

I went to China.

I went to America.

I crossed the Atlantic Ocean.

I crossed deserts.

I went to the North Pole.

I climbed to the top of Mount Everest.

I sailed a ship for 70 days.

Comparing explorers

How were the three explorers similar to each other? Read the sentences. Put ✓ in **two** boxes for each sentence. The first one has been done for you.

1 They crossed mountains.

[✓] [ ] [✓]

2 They sailed over oceans.

[ ] [ ] [ ]

3 They went to Asia.

[ ] [ ] [ ]

4 They lived more than 300 years ago.

[ ] [ ] [ ]

Remembering the three explorers

Stamps can help us remember people from the past. This stamp tells us about Christopher Columbus.

1 Design a stamp about **either** Ibn Battuta **or** Edmund Hillary.

2 Complete the sentences.

My stamp tells us about _____.

There is a picture of _____ on my stamp

because _____

_____.

Local history study

Find out about someone famous who was from your local area.
Complete the fact file.

What is the person's name?	
Draw a picture of the person.	
When was he or she born?	
Where was he or she born?	
Why is he or she famous?	
How do we remember him or her today?	

Three brave explorers

Complete the information for each explorer.

	Ibn Battuta	Christopher Columbus	Edmund Hillary
In which century did he live?			
Where was he born?			
Where did he explore?			
How did he travel?			
Why was he brave?			

Challenge

Who do you think was the most interesting explorer? Why have you chosen this explorer? Write your answers in your notebook.

Thinking about my learning

Learning outcome I can...	🙂	😐	☹️
describe the lives of three explorers.			
compare three different explorers.			
talk about different ways we remember the past.			

Three things I have learned...

1 _____

2 _____

3 _____

My favourite activity was...

_____

My favourite fact was...

_____

I would like to know more about...

_____

_____

Glossary

Write what each word means or draw a picture.

century

explorer

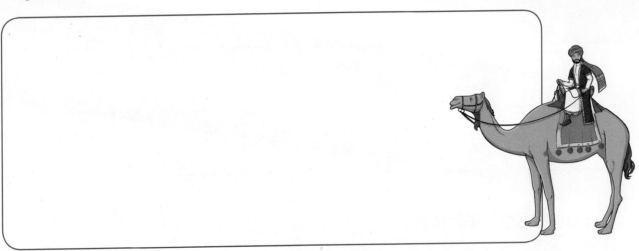

family tree

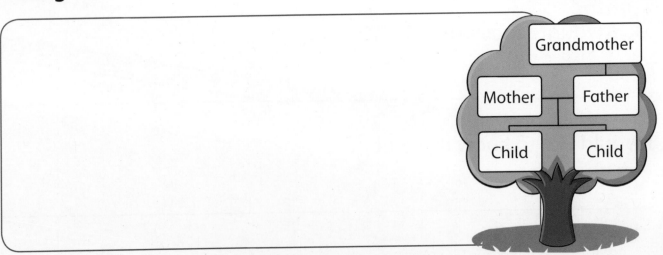

generation

history

invention

modern

the past

timeline

0 years – I was born.

1 year – I walked.

2 years – I kicked a ball.

3 years – My sister Laila was born.

4 years – I wrote my name.

5 years – I went to school.

voyage

North America

Spain   Europe

Atlantic Ocean

Italy

Africa

South America